Skyline 2

Resource Pack

Susan Banman Sileci

Ana Maria Cuder

MACMILLAN

Introduction

The *Skyline* Resource Pack contains thirty-six communicative activities for elementary students of English. It is designed to be used with Skyline Student's Book 2 but can be used to supplement any course.

The activities can be used for extension and consolidation purposes after target language is introduced, or be used later in the course as revision.

Teachers often ask about how to use resource packs. Here are some of the most frequently asked questions, together with answers.

Should I review target language with the class before students begin the activity?

There are different schools of thought. Some teachers argue that by not reviewing the language they have a better idea of which students can activate the language and which students need further help. Other teachers prefer to review the target language briefly in the hope that students will use it throughout the activity. There is no reason why a teacher cannot experiment with both approaches. If you decide to preview the target language, it is better to make it very brief, two to five minutes is usually enough. It may help less confident students to have a model of the target language on the board to refer to if they need it.

How do I teach students the rules for a game?

It's easier, and clearer to the students, if you show them how to play a game rather than explain the rules at length. One way is to model or show how the game works. Choose a student from the class to demonstrate the activity with you. It may not always be necessary to model the whole activity.

Students often want to speak in their mother tongue. How can I stop them?

Students speak in their mother tongue for a number of reasons. First they may not understand why they are doing an activity so it is helpful to explain the purpose and the final aim of an activity at the beginning. Second students may not understand what to do. Demonstrating the activity should resolve this problem by showing them what is expected of them. Finally students may also lack confidence or feel they do not have enough English to do the job properly. Modeling the task before the activity starts will enable students to be clear about the type of language they might use. Encouragement, as in everything, is also a very important motivational force.

What should I correct and when should I correct it?

This will depend on the aim of each activity. In general, it is helpful to limit areas of correction to the main aim of each activity. It may be that other areas of correction arise out of an activity. Many teachers find it helpful to note errors down under different categories while they are monitoring. Possible categories could be: target language, pronunciation or appropriacy of language use.

It is generally more productive not to stop students during an activity unless there is a breakdown in communication. Feedback can then take place directly after the activity or at a later point. It is important that students are given feedback on two areas: task performance and language performance.

Can I use these activities if my classes are very large or very small?

Yes, you can. If your class is large, try dividing it in half or in thirds. Each group then carries out the activity at the same time while you walk around and monitor the class. In this case, it's especially important to model the activity and make sure that students understand the procedures. If your class is small, some activities may need to be modified. For example, eliminate some cards or alter the rules to suit the circumstances.

What can I do to discourage students from looking at each other's worksheets or cue cards?

Most of the activities in the pack are based on the principle of an 'information gap' – that is, student A knows something that student B does not know, and vice versa. It's useful to explain this to students from the beginning of the course and tell them that when they look at each other's cue cards or worksheets it destroys the need to exchange information.

Students may also look at each other's information because they lack confidence in their English. It is helpful to stress that struggling to form questions or correct answers is a natural and useful part of the language learning process.

A further reason why students look at each other's material is because they aren't clear about how to do an activity. Careful demonstrating of an activity and constant encouragement should help. If there is enough space, students could sit face to face, or back to back.

Some students work more quickly than others. How can I handle this?

This situation is inevitable. Setting and keeping the time limits suggested in the activities can help, although your students may need more or less time. If the activity has two or more parts, make sure that a time limit is set for each part. If you find that some students always finish the activity before the set time limit, be prepared with an extra activity for them. Often the corresponding optional activity or additional activity in the Resource Packs can be used in these situations.

My students always seem to choose the same partners for pair work activities. Is this a good idea?

People tend to sit with people they like regardless of the type of class they are in but from a teacher's point of view it is better if students change partners. Sometimes it's helpful to explain the benefits of working with different people. For example, it improves rapport in the classroom and adds an element of interest and surprise to question and answer sequences. Students may then understand why they should change partners.

If your class is small, you could try keeping a small envelope with the names of every student on a piece of paper. Pull out two pieces of paper at a time and get these two students to be pairs for a particular activity. With larger classes, you can divide the class into two groups. Students on the the left side of the room will be students A in a pair work activity and the students on the right side will be students B. The left side then mixes with the right side and partners can be chosen accordingly. The next time, divide the class in half by front and back so students can't predict where you'll divide the room.

Should I monitor the activity if students are familiar with the grammar and know how the activity works?

Yes, most definitely. Monitoring is a very flexible teaching technique. Initially, many students feel nervous about having a teacher listen to them, but once that has disappeared they usually appreciate the attention. Monitoring offers you the chance to walk around the classroom and informally evaluate how well students are doing. You can give specific language input and encouragement to individuals and groups. It makes it easier to tackle the inevitable problem of students using their own language in the class too. At the same time it allows you to build a working relationship with individuals and smaller groups, which is something that is more difficult to do with larger classes. If you carry a pen and paper you can also note recurring problems for review at the next opportunity.

What do I do if there's an odd number of students in the class for pair work activities?

You can ask the extra student to model the activity with you for the rest of the class. Another possibility is to ask the extra student to work with a pair of students and either monitor that pair or take turns participating in the activity with them. Remember to rotate students if there's often an odd number so that the same student isn't the "extra" every time. It is not a good idea to participate in the activity yourself to make an even number of students, as this means that you are not free to walk around the classroom and monitor the activity.

It's expensive to make new photocopies every time. How can I save on this expense?

Some activities in the Resource Packs require students to use individual worksheets to answer questions about themselves or their partners. It's best to give fresh copies for this type of activity but, if necessary, you can ask students to write their answers on a separate piece of paper and collect the worksheets for re-use at another time. In some activities, where each student has a worksheet, you could write the information on the board and have students copy it into their notebooks before starting the activity. This way no photocopies are required.

There are many activities which require cutting cue cards or making game boards. For these activities, the same copies can be used over and over if you paste the cue cards or game boards to pieces of cardboard and store them carefully after the activity. Store each activity's copies in a separate envelope or plastic bag and write any necessary information on the outside of the envelope: name of activity, number of copies, number of players necessary or type of activity. Before using the same cards again, check that all the parts are still there so you don't start the activity with your class and only then find missing pairs or copies.

Contents

6A	A group story	Group work	To practice telling a story using the past simple and past progressive tenses.	15–20	Speaking	Review of verb tenses Connectors	General
6B	More about you	Pair work	To practice asking and answering questions. To practice sharing opinions.	20–25	Speaking Writing	Information questions and *yes / no* questions with the present simple and past simple	General
6C	Group literature	Group work	To practice writing, reading and speaking in the present simple, past simple and past progressive tenses.	15–20	Writing Reading Speaking	Review of present simple, past simple and past progressive tenses	Physical characteristics Dating
7A	Who is stronger?	Whole class	To compare abilities and physical attributes.	15–20	Speaking	Comparatives Asking and answering personal information questions	General
7B	Which one are you going to buy?	Pair work Whole class	To practice comparing different items.	20–25	Speaking	Comparatives Convincing someone of the superiority of a product Giving reasons	General
7C	Can you do me a favor?	Group work	To practice asking and answering questions using *can* and *could*.	20–25	Speaking	Asking someone for a favor Agreeing to do a favor	General verbs
8A	Incomplete history	Pair work	To practice asking questions using the past simple.	15–20	Speaking Reading	Past simple Asking and answering questions	General
8B	Do you agree?	Whole class	To practice using superlatives.	20–25	Speaking	Comparatives and superlatives Sharing opinions	General
8C	Where's the treasure?	Group work	To understand clues and find a hidden object.	20–25	Reading	Reading and using clues	Topographical points
9A	Pictionary	Group work	To review vocabulary learned in this and previous units.	20–25	Speaking	Guessing and defining words	General
9B	Who is it?	Pair work	To practice asking and answering questions about physical descriptions.	15–20	Speaking	Present simple in *yes / no* questions Asking and answering about people's physical characteristics	Physical characteristics
9C	They need advice!	Group work	To practice giving advice.	20–25	Speaking	Giving advice *Should / need to*	General
10A	Have you ever ...?	Group work	To practice using the present perfect with *ever*.	15–20	Speaking	Present perfect with *ever* Life experiences	General
10B	Bingo!	Whole class	To practice the past participle form of regular and irregular verbs.	15–20	Speaking	Past participle form of regular and irregular verbs	Infinitive and past participle form of verbs
10C	Snakes and ladders	Group work	To practice describing experiences in the present perfect.	25–30	Speaking	Present perfect Describing experiences	General
11A	Half a crossword	Pair work	To practice giving definitions.	20–25	Speaking	Questions in the present simple Defining words	Words from unit 11
11B	I've lived here since 1996	Group work	To practice the present perfect with *for* and *since*.	15–20	Speaking	Present perfect with *for* and *since* Talking about personal experiences	General
11C	Festival mix up	Group work	To practice reading and recognizing the present and past tenses.	15–20	Reading Speaking	Asking and answering about festivals and events	General
12A	Questions in a hat	Whole class	To practice the use of the modal auxiliary *will* to make predictions.	15–20	Writing Speaking	Modal auxiliary *will* Predicting the future	General
12B	I'm sure we've met!	Group work	To practice using the present perfect.	25–30	Reading Speaking	Present perfect and the past simple	General
12C	Time travelers	Group work	To practice differentiating between modal auxiliaries *will* and *might*.	20–25	Speaking	Modal auxiliaries *will* and *might* Sharing opinions	General

Guggenheim

Interaction
Group work

Aim
To review and activate vocabulary from Skyline 1.

Time
25–30 minutes

Skills
Speaking

Grammar and functions
Present simple
Asking for specific information

Vocabulary
Countries
Kinds of food
Occupations
Leisure-time activities
Verbs
The alphabet

Preparation
Photocopy and cut apart the cards. Make sure you have a copy of each card for every student.

Procedure

1 Write the word *food* on the board. Elicit and write the names of different foods on the board.

2 Divide the class into groups of five. Give each student a copy of the first Guggenheim card. Check that they understand each category.

3 Explain how to play the game.
   • Each student thinks of seven countries that begin with each of the seven letters in the word ENGLISH and writes them in the correct spaces. Students then do the same with the other categories, e.g.

	A country	A sport	A food
E	Ethiopia	Equitation	Egg
N	Nicaragua	Netball	Nut

   • Students must not show their cards to their classmates.
   • When everyone has finished, have the groups compare the names on their cards.
   • One point is given for answers which no one else has thought of. The winner is the student with the most points.

4 Give students five minutes to fill in their tables.

5 Ask students to compare their answers in their groups. Beforehand, elicit questions they could ask each other and write them on the board, e.g. *What's a sport that starts with G?*

6 As students compare answers, walk around the classroom and check their answers.

7 Ask the winner to read his / her answers aloud.

8 Hand out the next card and repeat the steps.

Additional ideas
Give students the blank cards and have students make their own cards. Make it clear that students should be able to think of answers to all the categories. When students have finished, collect their cards, shuffle them and give them out again, one to each group in the class. Follow the steps above.

Guggenheim

	A country	A sport	A food
E			
N			
G			
L			
I			
S			
H			

--✂

	A verb	A city	An occupation
C			
O			
U			
N			
T			
R			
Y			

--✂

Tell me about yourself

Interaction
Pair work

Aim
To practice asking for and giving personal information.

Time
15–20 minutes

Skills
Speaking

Grammar and functions
Present simple
Question words

Vocabulary
Occupations
Hobbies and leisure-time activities
Adjectives

Preparation
Photocopy and cut apart the A / B cards. Make sure you have one A / B set for every pair of students in the class.

Procedure
1 Divide the class into two groups: A and B.
2 Give an A card to every student in group A and a B card to every student in group B.
3 Explain the task. Students work in pairs and complete their forms by talking to each other.
4 Go through all the items on students' cards and explain any new words to them.
5 Elicit the questions students are going to ask each other. If necessary, write them on the board, e.g. *What's your full name? Why are you studying English? Do you have any hobbies? What are they?*
6 Play the part of a student A and model the activity with a student B.
7 Set a time limit of ten minutes and ask students to do the activity in A / B pairs.
8 Move around the room and give help as needed.
9 When the time is up, invite several students to introduce their partners to the class.

Option
Ask students to work individually and complete the charts with what they imagine their colleagues will answer or what they remember about their partners from last semester. Have students check their guesses with their partners by asking and answering about the items on the cards.

Additional ideas
Ask students to write a paragraph about their partners, omitting their names. Display the paragraphs on a wall or read them aloud to the class. Ask students to guess the name of the person described.

Tell me about yourself

Student A

Full name:
Hometown:
Reason for studying English:
Occupation / Subject of study:
Musical instruments he / she plays:
Favorite movies:
Favorite singers / bands:
Leisure-time activities:
Main goal in life:
Three adjectives to describe himself / herself:
One city he / she wants to visit this year:

✂

Student B

Full name:
Hometown:
Reason for studying English:
Occupation / Subject of study:
Hobbies:
Favorite TV shows:
Favorite magazines:
Languages he / she speaks:
Main goal in life:
Three adjectives to describe himself / herself:
One new activity he / she wants to learn this year:

Find your place

Interaction
Group work

Aim
To practice asking and answering information questions in the present simple.

Time
10–15 minutes

Skills
Reading

Grammar and functions
Present simple in information questions
Checking in to a hotel
Confirming hotel reservations

Vocabulary
Types of rooms in a hotel
Payment methods

Preparation
Photocopy and cut apart the eleven sentence cards and shuffle them. Make one complete set for every group of eleven students in the class.

Answers

The conversation is in the correct order on the activity sheet.

Procedure

1   Divide the class into groups of eleven.

2   Give each student in the group a sentence card. If you have fewer than eleven students, give more than one card to several students, making sure that the cards given to one student are next to one another on the worksheet, e.g. give the first two sentences to one student and the next two to another. If you have more than eleven students, divide the class into two or more groups.

3   Give students time to read their lines.

4   Explain the task. Students read their lines aloud, one at a time, and reconstruct the conversation by lining up in the correct order.

5   Set a time limit of ten minutes. Ask students to start the activity.

6   Move around the room and give help if it is needed.

7   When the time is up or when the students have finished, check their answers by asking groups to read their lines aloud.

8   Ask groups which have correctly put their sentences in order to help those that have not, until all the groups have put their sentences in order.

Option
Divide the class into groups of four or five students. Give a complete set of sentences to each group and ask them to reconstruct the conversation while sitting at their desks. If possible, have them glue or staple the conversation to a piece of paper so it can be checked later on.

Additional ideas
Ask students to work in pairs and role play the conversation, using their own names and information about themselves.

Find your place

Good morning! May I help you?

Yes, I have a reservation for a single room.

What's your name?

Jack Steinfeltz.

Steinfeltz ... Steinfeltz ... yes here you are. One non-smoking single room.

Great. What room number is it?

It's room number 512. How would you like to pay? Cash or charge?

Charge, please. Do you accept visa?

Yes, we do. MasterCard too.

Fine. Here's my card and thank you very much.

Thank you, Mr Steinfeltz. Have a nice stay!

Skyline Resource Pack 2. Published by Macmillan Publishers Limited.

City trivia

Interaction
Group work

Aim
To practice the present simple.

Time
10–15 minutes

Skills
Speaking

Grammar and functions
Information questions and answers in the present simple

Vocabulary
Countries
Capital cities
Landmarks

Preparation
Photocopy, cut apart and shuffle the cards. Make sure you have one complete set for each group of six students.

Answers

The sentences are in the correct order on the activity page.

Procedure

1 Ask students some general questions about geography, e.g.
   Where is the statue of Liberty? (New York)
   What is the capital of England? (London)

2 Divide the class into groups of six.

3 Give each group a complete set of cards and tell them that they are going to play a game to test their geographical knowledge.

4 Explain the task. Students have to match the phrases in order to make 15 correct sentences.

5 Set a time limit of ten minutes and ask students to begin the task in their groups.

6 When the time is up, check their sentences.

7 The group with the most correct sentences wins.

Option
Give one incomplete card to each student in the class. Ask students to move around the class asking and answering other students until they find the other half of their card, e.g
A: *What does your card say?*
B: *My card says China.*
A: *Oh, sorry but I need something else.*

Additional ideas
Students work in groups and write a paragraph about their city or country. They could include interesting facts, population size, vacation spots and landmarks.

City trivia

The Eiffel Tower is in	Paris, France.
The Coca-Cola headquarters is in	Atlanta, U.S.
The city of Sydney, Australia is	on the beach.
Hollywood is in	Los Angeles, U.S.
Mexico City has the highest	population in the world.
The Golden Gate Bridge is in	San Francisco, U.S.
Reykjavik is the capital of	Iceland.
Beijing is the capital of	China.
The Kremlin is in	Moscow, Russia.
The Petrona Towers buildings are in	Kuala Lumpur, Malaysia.
Jerusalem is the capital of	Israel.
Damascus is the capital of	Syria.
The 2000 summer Olympics were in	Sydney, Australia.
Big Ben is in	London, England.
The United Nations headquarters is in	New York City, U.S.

Office crossword

Interaction
Pair work

Aim
To practice giving definitions.

Time
15–20 minutes

Skills
Speaking

Grammar and functions
Asking for and giving definitions

Vocabulary
Office equipment and supplies

Preparation
Photocopy and cut apart the A / B cards. Make one copy for each pair of students in the class.

Answers

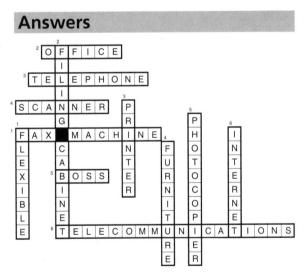

Procedure

1 Give half the class student A cards and the other half student B cards.

2 Divide the students into A / B pairs.

3 Explain the task. Both students in each pair have an incomplete crossword puzzle. Students have to complete it by asking each other questions. They should give each other definitions and they must not tell their partner the word.

4 Elicit the type of questions and answers students are going to need and write them on the board, e.g.
Student A: *What's number 2 across?*
Student B: *It's a place where executives and secretaries work.*

5 Set a time limit of ten minutes and ask students to begin the activity in their pairs.

6 Move around the room and give help if it is needed.

7 When the time is up ask students to compare their crossword puzzles and check their answers.

Option
Before students begin the activity, ask them to work in pairs or small groups of A or B students. Get them to check the meanings of all the words in their crossword puzzle and practice giving definitions. Students can write their definitions on the lines to the right of their crossword. Then divide students into A / B pairs to complete the crossword puzzles.

Office crossword

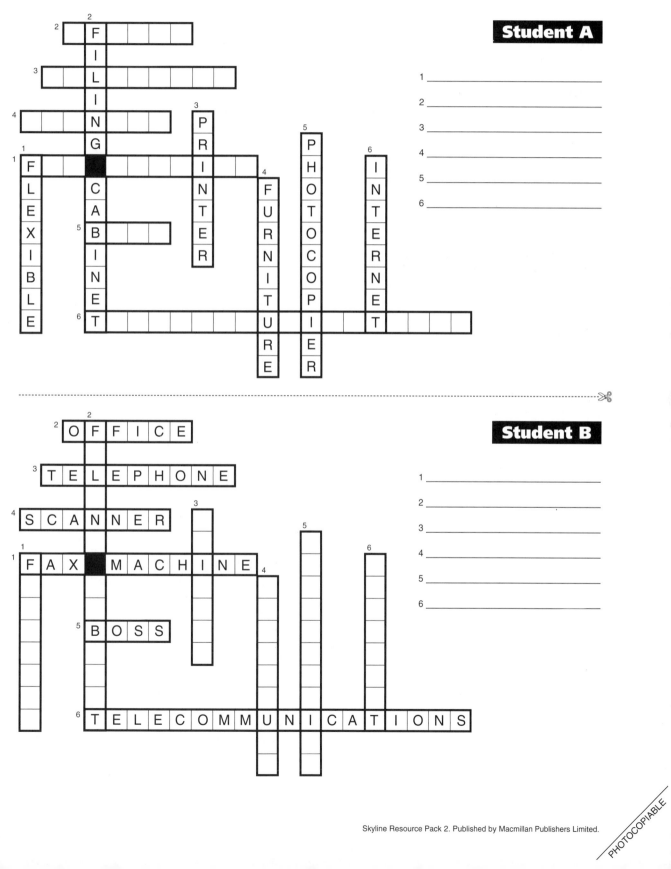

Student A

1 _____

2 _____

3 _____

4 _____

5 _____

6 _____

Student B

1 _____

2 _____

3 _____

4 _____

5 _____

6 _____

Group predictions

Interaction
Group work

Aim
To share opinions and ideas about urban life.

Time
20–25 minutes

Skills
Reading
Speaking

Grammar and functions
Asking and answering questions about preferences
Information questions and *yes / no* questions in
the present simple

Vocabulary
Lifestyles
Cities

Preparation
Photocopy the worksheets. Make sure you have
one for each student in the class.

Procedure
1   Divide the class into groups of four.

2   Give each student a worksheet.

3   Ask students to write the names of their three
partners in the spaces provided.

4   Explain the task. Individually, students read
the questions and check the alternative that
best coincides with their opinion. When
students have finished this, they guess their
partners' answers to those questions and write
them in the spaces provided.

5   Set a time limit of ten minutes and ask
students to begin the task.

6   When the time is up explain the task for the
second part of the activity. Students check
with the members of their groups to see
whether their guesses are right or wrong and
discuss their answers.

7   Set a time limit of ten minutes and ask
students to finish the activity.

8   Move around the room and give help if needed.

9   When the time is up invite some students to
report their conclusions to the class.

Option
Ask students to check how many correct guesses
they have. The student with the most correct
guesses wins the game.

Additional ideas
Ask students to form pairs. Make a list of topics on
the board, e.g. *marital status, work, study, trips
to other countries, free time activities, sports.*
Get each pair to agree on a subject. Individually,
each student should use that topic as a guideline
to write five sentences about his / her partner, e.g.
*I think my partner wants to get married soon. I
think he wants to marry a very pretty woman.
He wants his wife to stay at home.* Students
should then check the accuracy of their guesses
by talking to each other and discussing what they
have written about.

Group predictions

	You			
On Saturday nights, I usually: • stay at home with my family. • go to a quiet restaurant with friends. • go to an exciting disco. • other				
My idea of a perfect city is: • a metropolis like New York City. • a mid-sized city of 500,000 inhabitants. • a small town with under 5000 inhabitants. • other				
For me, the ideal place to live is: • downtown. • in the suburbs. • in the country. • other				
The ideal place for children to live is: • downtown. • in the suburbs. • in the country. • other				
An important element to have in a city is: • low pollution. • tourist attractions. • honest government. • other				
A good place for a university is: • in a small, residential town. • in a large, busy city. • in a quiet, commercial city. • other				
A big problem for my city is: • crime. • pollution. • corruption. • other				
My ideal city has: • lots of historic buildings and interesting architecture. • beaches and hot weather. • an honest, hard-working government and good public services. • other				

What does that represent?

Interaction
Group work

Aim
To practice asking and answering personal information questions.

Time
25–30 minutes

Skills
Speaking

Grammar and functions
Present simple with information and *yes / no* questions
Giving personal information

Vocabulary
Age
Colors
Occupations
Family members

Preparation
Photocopy and cut apart the six cards. Make sure you have one card for each student in the class.

Procedure

1   Divide the class into groups of six. If you have more students, divide them into groups of five.

2   Explain the first part of the game. Each student will have a different card on which they will see questions and a space for answers. They have to write short answers to each question; just a number or word where possible. They must write their names at the top of the second column.

3   Give students five minutes to do this.

4   Explain the next part of the game. Students tear the answers from the questions and put their answer cards face up on the table, keeping the questions hidden.

5   Give students a couple of minutes to do this.

6   Explain the final part of the game. Group members choose one card and try to discover what the answers refer to by asking questions to the person who wrote the answers, e.g. If the answer were *6*:
Group: *Do you have six cousins?*
Student: *No, I don't. I have three.*
Group: *Do you have six uncles?*
Student: *Yes that's right.*

7   The game continues until all cards have been used.

Option
Ask students to write complete answers to the questions, but omit their names, e.g.
My eyes are blue. I have three brothers.
Students cut off the questions from the answers and give you the answer cards. Shuffle the answer cards and distribute them. Ask students to move around the class asking questions until they find the person who wrote those answers.

Additional ideas
Get students to write complete answers to the questions, but omit their names, e.g.
I have six cousins. My favorite movie is Matrix.
Collect all the cards and shuffle them. Read a card and ask students to guess who wrote the answers.

Skyline Resource Pack 2. Published by Macmillan Publishers Limited.

What does that represent?

Question	Name:
How many brothers do you have?	
What color are your eyes?	
What are two adjectives that describe you?	

Question	Name:
What number is your house or apartment?	
What's your favorite color?	
What's your middle name?	

Question	Name:
What city do you want to visit on your next vacation?	
How many cousins do you have?	
What's your favorite movie?	

Question	Name:
What's your occupation?	
What's your favorite holiday?	
How many people are there in your family?	

Question	Name:
What are the initials of your favorite movie star?	
What color is your hair?	
How many sisters do you have?	

Question	Name:
How old are you?	
What's a country you don't want to visit?	
What are two things you can do very well?	

Skyline Resource Pack 2. Published by Macmillan Publishers Limited.

Who am I talking about?

Interaction
Team work

Aim
To practice describing people.

Time
20–25 minutes

Skills
Speaking

Grammar and functions
Describing someone's physical characteristics, occupation, nationality and age

Vocabulary
Words related to physical description
Occupations
Nationalities
Numbers

Preparation
Photocopy and cut apart the name cards.

Procedure

1   Divide the class into two teams: A and B. If the class is large, divide the class into groups of 6 or 8 and then divide those groups into teams. Play the game in each group simultaneously, so that more students can participate. (In this case you will need one set of cards for each group.)

2   Shuffle the cards and place them face down on a table.

3   Explain the task. Taking turns, one person from each team comes to the front of the class, chooses a card and describes that person to his / her team. Team members guess the name of the person in the shortest time possible.

4   Play a trial game with the students. Think of a famous person and describe him / her to the students. Ask them to guess who it is.

5   Write some key words on the board to help students, e.g. *man / woman / age / hair color / nationality / famous for ___ .*

6   Start the game. Taking turns, one student from each team picks a card and describes that person to his / her team.

7   Make sure the student who describes a person is different each time, so that more students get the opportunity to practice.

Option
Divide the class into groups of five or six and ask each group to choose a representative. Give each representative a set of five cards and allow them a few minutes to familiarize themselves with the names. Taking turns, have the representatives describe the people to their teams. Set a time limit of three minutes for each representative. The group with most correct guesses wins.

Additional ideas
Give each student a card and say that they should pretend to be that person. Students then work in pairs and ask their partners *yes / no* questions in order to guess who they are.

Who am I talking about?

Madonna	Pelé	Michael Jordan
Eddie Murphy	Quentin Tarantino	**Fidel Castro**
Queen Elizabeth II	**Fred Flintstone**	**Mick Jagger**
Tina Turner	**Bill Gates**	Jackie Chan
Mohammed Ali	**Denzel Washington**	Jennifer Lopez
Enrique Iglesias	Woody Allen	Bugs Bunny
Britney Spears	Michael Schumacher	Barbie
Ricky Martin	***Steven Spielberg***	Carlos Santana
Tom Cruise	Superman	Julia Roberts
Stephen King	Hillary Clinton	**Brad Pitt**

Skyline Resource Pack 2. Published by Macmillan Publishers Limited.

Wedding invitation

Interaction
Pair work

Aims
To practice talking about weddings.
To practice dates and times.
To practice different ways of addressing people.

Time
10–15 minutes

Skills
Reading
Speaking

Grammar and functions
Talking about weddings
Reading invitations

Vocabulary
Weddings

Preparation
Photocopy the worksheet. Make one copy for each pair of students in the class.

Answers

1 It should be Mrs. Arthur Taylor not Miss Taylor.
2 The daughter can't be named Robert Anne.
3 There are only 28 or 29 days in February.
4 ... half past quarter to eight o'clock is not a possible time.
5 There is no St. Stephanie.
6 North South East West 14th Street is not a possible address.
7 Los Angeles is in the state of California, not Florida.

Procedure

1 Introduce the topic. Ask class members some questions about weddings and initiate a short discussion, e.g. *Are you married?*
If the answer is *yes,* ask about the wedding ceremony, e.g. *Where was it? When was it?*

2 Explain the activity. Students work in pairs and read the invitation to find the mistakes.

3 Do not tell the students that there are seven mistakes. Tell them only that they should read the invitation with their partners and find all the mistakes they can.

4 Give one worksheet to each pair.

5 Ask students to begin the activity and tell them they have five minutes to find the mistakes.

6 After five minutes stop the activity and tell students that there are seven mistakes in the invitation. Give the pairs two more minutes to make sure they've found the seven mistakes.

7 Check the answers by asking one pair to tell you one mistake they have found. Make sure all students agree and then ask another pair to tell you another mistake. Continue checking the answers like this until all seven mistakes have been found and discussed.

Additional ideas
Ask students to compare the invitation on the worksheet, a standard invitation from the U.S., with invitations from their countries. Have students discuss the differences between weddings in the U.S. and weddings in their native country.

Wedding invitation

Mr. and Miss Arthur Taylor
request the honor of your presence at the marriage of their daughter

Robert Anne

to

Mr. David Williams, Jr.

on Saturday, the thirtieth of February
at half past quarter to eight o'clock

St. Stephanie Church
1156 North South East West 14th Street
Los Angeles, Florida

You're washing a giraffe!

Interaction
Team work

Aim
To practice using the present progressive.

Time
20–30 minutes

Skills
Speaking

Grammar and functions
Information questions in the present progressive

Vocabulary
Action verbs

Preparation
Photocopy and cut apart the cards. Make one set for the class.

Procedure

1   Divide the students into two teams: A and B. If the class is large, divide the class into groups of 6 or 8 and then divide those groups into teams. Play the game in each group simultaneously, so that more students have a chance to participate. (In this case you will need one set of cards for each group.)

2   Explain the activity. Taking turns, one student from each team comes to the front of the class, chooses a sentence card and mimes the action described on that card to his / her team. Team members try to guess the action by asking *yes / no* questions, e.g.
A: *Are you climbing a tree?*
B: *No, I'm not.*
C: *Are you climbing stairs?*
B: *Yes, I am!*

3   Play the activity once with the whole class, to make sure they understand what they are supposed to do.

4   Place the cards face down on a table.

5   Throw a coin to decide which team starts.

6   Set a time limit of about 10 or 15 minutes and start the game.

7   Make sure a different student does the miming on each turn.

Option
Make the game more competitive by timing the activity. Give each team thirty seconds to guess the action being mimed. The team with the most correct guesses, after a set amount of time, wins.

Additional ideas
In addition to using the actions listed on the worksheet, ask the students to write their own actions.

You're washing a giraffe!

You're sitting in a boat on the ocean.	You're riding a roller coaster.
You're a fireman.	You're reading a letter with bad news.
You're feeding meat to a lion.	You're sending a fax.
You're a fashion model.	You're having a birthday party.
You're opening an alligator's mouth.	You're giving a baby some food.
You're looking at paintings in a museum.	You're making a snowman.
You're buying tickets to a movie.	You're climbing a tree to save a cat.
You're watching a soccer game.	You're taking five dogs for a walk.
You're in prison.	You're sitting in traffic.
You're climbing a mountain.	You're robbing a bank.
You're falling in love.	You're walking on the moon.
You're pushing an old man in a wheelchair.	You're fixing a broken plate.
You're playing the trumpet in a parade.	You're catching a big fish.
You're eating a delicious dessert.	You're watching a horror movie.

Find three people who ...

Interaction
Whole class

Aim
To practice asking and answering about habits, hobbies and routines.

Time
30–40 minutes

Skills
Speaking

Grammar and functions
Information questions in the present simple
Adverbs of frequency

Vocabulary
Hobbies
Daily routine
Leisure-time activities

Preparation
Photocopy the worksheets. Make one copy for each student in the class.

Procedure

1 Give one worksheet to each student.

2 Explain the task. Students move around the room asking questions until they find three people who do each of the things listed on their worksheets. Encourage students to find out extra information about students who do the things listed.

3 Allow students a few minutes to familiarize themselves with the information on the worksheet and answer any questions they might have about vocabulary.

4 Elicit the kind of questions they are going to ask. If necessary, write them on the board, e.g. *Do you go to church? How often do you go to church? Do you think that shopping is relaxing? Why?*

5 Set a time limit of about ten minutes and ask students to start the task.

6 When the time is up, check students' answers. Invite several students to report their conclusions to the class, e.g.
Student: *Both Marcelo and Monica are going to take a vacation abroad next year.*
Teacher: *Where is Marcelo going to go?*
Student: *He's going to go to Canada.*

Option
Ask students to use the activity as a competition. Instead of finding three people who can answer affirmatively to each of the ideas on the worksheet, students should interview different classmates and collect as many names as they can within ten minutes. The student with the most names wins.

Additional ideas
Photocopy the worksheet and cut apart the different cards. Make sure there's one card for each student. Proceed with the activity as outlined in the procedure section above. Students only need to find three people who answer affirmatively to the question on their card, they do not need to complete the whole worksheet.

Skyline Resource Pack 2. Published by Macmillan Publishers Limited.

Find three people who ...

	Find three people who usually go to church on Sundays.		Find three people who fall in love twice a year.
	Find three people who believe men should share 50% of the housework.		Find three people who usually sleep for eight hours every night.
	Find three people who believe that men and women can't be friends.		Find three people who are going to try to change this year.
	Find three people who always receive approximately 20 business e-mails a day.		Find three people who think that going shopping is relaxing.
	Find three people who often watch at least two hours of TV a day.		Find three people who never exercise.
	Find three people who prefer reading books to watching TV.		Find three people who usually work over 12 hours a day.
	Find three people who are going to take a vacation abroad this year.		Find three people who have great bosses.

Skyline Resource Pack 2. Published by Macmillan Publishers Limited.

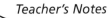

Coffeepot

Interaction
Team work

Aim
To review using the present simple and present progressive tenses.

Time
20–25 minutes

Skills
Speaking

Grammar and functions
Yes / no questions
Present simple and present progressive tenses

Vocabulary
Action verbs

Preparation
Photocopy and cut apart the action cards. Only one set is necessary for the class.

Procedure
1 Divide the class into two teams: A and B.
2 Place the action cards face down on a table.
3 Explain the activity.
   - Taking turns, a student from each team comes to the front of the class and picks up a card.
   - The students from his / her team have to ask *yes / no* questions to guess the action on the card.
   - Students' sentences should include the word *coffeepot* in the place of the unknown verb, e.g. *Do you coffeepot everyday? Do women coffeepot? Are you coffeepotting now?*
   - Students have one minute to ask as many questions as they can and guess the action.
   - If students guess the action correctly then they win a point.
   - The team with the most points wins.
4 Choose an action yourself and play a trial game with the students to make sure they understand exactly what they are supposed to do.
5 Set a time limit of fifteen minutes and ask students to play the game.
6 Make sure that a different student comes to the front of the classroom each time.

Option
Instead of playing the game in teams, ask students to play the game in groups or pairs.

Additional ideas
The student who comes to the front of the class can choose to answer information questions as well, e.g.
Class: *What time of the day do you coffeepot?*
Student: *Usually in the morning but sometimes at night.*
Class: *How often do you coffeepot?*
Student: *Every day, if I can.*

Coffeepot

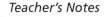

Party people!

Interaction
Pair work

Aim
To practice asking and answering questions with *there is / there are*.

Time
10–15 minutes

Skills
Speaking

Grammar and functions
There is / there are
Some / any / no
Comparing objects in a room

Vocabulary
Living room furniture
Party words

Preparation
Photocopy and cut apart the A / B cards. Make sure you have one complete set for each pair of students in the class.

Answers

Picture A
1 There are six sandwiches on a plate on the buffet table.
2 There are four cans of soda on the buffet table.
3 There are eleven CDs by the stereo.
4 There are three wine glasses by the wine bottle.
5 There is a bowl of peanuts on the table near the wine.
6 There is a couple dancing.

Picture B
1 There are five sandwiches on a plate on the buffet table.
2 There are five cans of soda on the buffet table.
3 There are eight CDs by the stereo.
4 There is one wine glass by the wine bottle.
5 There are no peanuts on the table near the wine.
6 There is a woman playing the guitar and a man singing. They are standing together.

Procedure
1 Give half the class student A cards and the other half student B cards.

2 Divide the class into A / B pairs.

3 Explain the task. Tell students that student A's card shows a picture of a party and student B's card shows a similar picture of the same party. However, there are six differences between the two pictures. The object of the game is for the pairs to find the six differences by asking each other questions.

4 Elicit the kind of questions they are going to ask, e.g. *How many bottles are there on the table? Is there a cake in your picture?*

5 Play the part of a student A and model the activity with a student B.

6 Set a time limit of ten minutes and get students to start the activity.

7 Go around checking that students are not simply comparing their pictures.

8 When the time is up, stop the activity and check students' answers.

Additional ideas
When students have finished asking and answering questions, ask them to write a short paragraph comparing the two pictures.

Party people!

I think my partner ...

Interaction
Pair work

Aims
To practice the present simple.
To practice sharing opinions.

Time
20–25 minutes

Skills
Speaking

Grammar and functions
Information questions in the present simple
Talking about one's likes, dislikes and habits
Giving opinions
Justifying choices

Vocabulary
Likes and dislikes
Habits and daily routines

Preparation
Photocopy and cut apart the A / B cards so that there is one set for each pair of students.

Procedure
1   Give half the group student A cards and the other half student B cards.

2   Allow the students a few minutes to familiarize themselves with the information on their cards. You may want to pre-teach the words below.
Extreme sports – sports that are unusually dangerous, e.g. *parachuting*.
To flirt – to behave playfully, usually to attract the attention of someone of the opposite sex.
To be afraid of – to be anxious, to be scared.
Charity – an organization that helps people / animals in need.

3   Ask students to form A / B pairs and explain the first part of the activity. Students read the questions on their card and circle an answer that they think best corresponds to their partner. Give examples using yourself as the model, e.g. *How well do you know me? Do I like eating out? Yes or No? Am I afraid of insects? Yes or No?*

4   Set a time limit of five minutes. Make sure students do the task individually.

5   Explain the task for the second part of the activity. Students talk to their partners and check whether their guesses were correct.

6   Set a time limit of ten minutes and ask students to start checking their guesses.

7   When the time is up, check how many correct guesses students made and who knew their partner the best.

8   Invite several students to report their right / wrong guesses to the class.

Option
Ask students to work in groups of six. Give three students card A and the other three card B. Have students read the questions and guess who in the group would fit in the *Yes* column and who would fit in the *No* column and write the students' names in those spaces. Then ask the groups to check whether their guesses were right or wrong.

I think my partner ...

Student A

I think my partner ...	Yes	No	Right or Wrong?
is interested in practicing extreme sports.			
likes eating rice and beans.			
likes to flirt.			
is going to be an excellent English speaker in one year.			
sings in the shower.			
watches a lot of TV.			
is afraid of airplanes.			
gives to charity.			
doesn't like pets.			
likes heavy metal.			
likes eating in restaurants.			
is a good singer.			

---✂

Student B

I think my partner ...	Yes	No	Right or Wrong?
is afraid of insects.			
believes in God.			
likes children.			
is a good dancer.			
likes speaking in public.			
likes action movies.			
exercises three times a week.			
always eats a big breakfast.			
prefers staying at home on the weekends.			
wants to live in another country.			
likes fashionable clothes.			
likes looking in the mirror.			

Skyline Resource Pack 2. Published by Macmillan Publishers Limited.

What's on TV?

Interaction
Pair work

Aim
To practice the present simple.

Time
15–20 minutes

Skills
Reading
Speaking

Grammar and functions
Using the present simple to talk about TV shows
Asking for and giving times

Vocabulary
Types of TV shows

Preparation
Photocopy the worksheet. Make sure you have one copy for each pair of students in the class.

Procedure

1 Give half the class student A cards and the other half student B cards.

2 Divide the class into A / B pairs.

3 Explain that each student has part of a TV guide and that, working in pairs, they should ask and answer questions to complete their guides.

4 Elicit possible questions from the students and write them on the board if necessary, e.g. *What's on Channel 2 at 10:00? What time is Up the River on?*

5 Ask students to begin the activity. Walk around the class and give help as necessary.

6 After ten minutes, ask students to compare their TV guides to check their answers.

Option
Ask students to look at the TV guide with their partners and decide what they would like to watch. Get them to discuss what types of programs there are and what the different programs could be about.

Answers

Start time	Program	Length	Channel
9:00	**Movie:** Space World	2hrs	2
	Documentary: New York - A complete History	1hr	4
	Comedy: Bergfeld Blues	30mins	5
9:30	**Cartoon:** Goofy the Goose	30mins	3
	Comedy: Jane's World	1hr	5
	Music: Blues in New Orleans	30mins	9
10:00	**Drama:** Up the River	1hr	3
	Documentary: Famous Crocodiles of The Outback	30mins	4
	News: The 10:00 News with Mark Higgins	30mins	11
10:30	**Comedy:** That's Not My Dad!	30mins	5
	Music: The Rock Dance Show with Dick Hark	45mins	9
	Game show: Making Millions!	30mins	10
11:00	**Movie:** The Last Train to London	2hrs 30mins	2
	Comedy: Baby's Bath!	30mins	3
	Documentary: Japanese Festivals	30mins	4

What's on TV?

Student A

Start time	Program	Length	Channel
9:00	**Movie:** Space World		2
	Documentary: New York - A complete History	1hr	
	Comedy: Bergfeld Blues	30mins	5
9:30		30mins	3
	Comedy: Jane's World	1hr	5
	Music: Blues in New Orleans	30mins	9
10:00	**Drama:** Up the River		3
	Documentary: Famous Crocodiles of The Outback	30mins	4
		30mins	11
10:30	**Comedy:** That's Not My Dad!	30mins	5
	Music: The Rock Dance Show with Dick Hark	45mins	
	Game show: Making Millions!		10
11:00		2hrs 30mins	2
	Comedy: Baby's Bath!		3
	Documentary: Japanese Festivals	30mins	4

--- ✀

Student B

Start time	Program	Length	Channel
9:00		2hrs	2
	Documentary: New York - A complete History	1hr	4
			5
9:30	**Cartoon:** Goofy the Goose		3
	Comedy: Jane's World	1hr	
	Music: Blues in New Orleans	30mins	9
10:00	**Drama:** Up the River	1hr	3
	Documentary: Famous Crocodiles of The Outback		4
	News: The 10:00 News with Mark Higgins	30mins	11
10:30	**Comedy:** That's Not My Dad!		5
	Music: The Rock Dance Show with Dick Hark	45mins	9
	Game show: Making Millions!	30mins	10
11:00	**Movie:** The Last Train to London		2
		30mins	
	Documentary: Japanese Festivals	30mins	4

A group story

Interaction
Group work

Aim
To practice telling a story using the past simple and past progressive tenses.

Time
15–20 minutes

Skills
Speaking

Grammar and functions
Review of verb tenses
Connectors

Vocabulary
General

Preparation
Photocopy and cut apart the cards. Make sure you have one complete set for each group of students in the class.

Procedure

1 Divide the class into groups of five.

2 Give a complete set of cards to each group and ask students to take four cards each.

3 Give them one or two minutes to familiarize themselves with the words and pictures on their cards. You might want to pre-teach the words below.
To growl – make a low, unfriendly sound (especially dogs).
A mask – a covering for the face.
Windy – an adjective to describe a road or way that is not straight.
A rope – a thick length of material used for tying things.
Animal print – the mark an animal makes in the ground with its feet.
Wood / Forest – an area with lots of trees.

4 Explain the task. In their groups, students should build up a story. All the students in the group should contribute to the story by using the words or pictures on their cards.

5 Remind students that the story should have a coherent sequence of events and that it should only end when the students have no cards left.

6 Set a time limit of ten minutes and ask students to start the activity.

7 Move around the room and give help as needed.

8 When the time is up, invite one member from each team to retell their story to the class.

Option
As a whole class activity, ask students to sit in a circle. Give one card to each student. Start telling a story and point to a student to continue. Go on doing so until all the students have contributed to the story, using their card to help them.

Additional ideas
After each group has finished its story, ask students to write down the main ideas of the story in a clear, coherent form.

A group story

More about you

Interaction
Pair work

Aims
To practice asking and answering questions.
To practice sharing opinions.

Time
20–25 minutes

Skills
Speaking
Writing

Grammar and functions
Information questions and *yes / no* questions with the present simple and past simple.

Vocabulary
General

Preparation
Photocopy and cut apart the A / B cards. Make sure you have a complete A / B set for every pair of students in the class.

Procedure
1 Give half the class student A cards and the other half student B cards.
2 Divide the class into A / B pairs.
3 Explain that the students need to ask their partners questions in order to fill out their charts.
4 Read two or three lines from each card and elicit the answers from around the class.
5 Play the part of a student A and model the activity with a student B.
6 Set a time limit of ten minutes for the first part of the activity. Ask students to do the activity in A / B pairs, with student A asking questions and noting his / her partner's answers.
7 When the time is up, ask students to change roles. This time, student B should ask the questions and note his / her partner's answers. Set a time limit of ten minutes.
8 When the time is up, invite individual students to tell the class what they found out about their partners.

Option
Ask students to work individually and guess their partner's answers to the questions on their charts. Then have students work in pairs and check their guesses to find out how well they know their partners.

Additional ideas
After finishing the activity as outlined in the procedure section above, ask students to write three or four sentences about their partner on a piece of paper, omitting their partners' names. Collect the papers, shuffle them and give them out, one to each student in the class. Students move around the class asking questions until they find the person their paper describes. The first student to find the person their paper describes, is the winner.

More about you

Find out if student A ...	Yes	No	Additional Information
thinks there's too much sex and violence on TV.			
lives in an apartment.			
has a bicycle.			
was dancing at a disco last night.			
was robbed last year.			
wants to get married some day.			
thinks the Internet has improved the world.			
was watching TV last night at 10:00 p.m.			
drove above the speed limit some time this week.			
traveled abroad last year.			
had a headache some time this week.			
is happy at his / her job or school.			
has a gun.			
saw a good movie last weekend.			

- ✂

Find out if student B ...	Yes	No	Additional Information
was sleeping this morning at 7:00 a.m.			
rented a video last night.			
was ill in the last month.			
lives with his / her family.			
was in love some time last year.			
felt stressed yesterday.			
enjoys learning English.			
thinks making money is very important in life.			
has more than ten pairs of shoes.			
thinks people should give money to beggars.			
has a motorcycle.			
knows how to clean a fish.			
read a good magazine article last week.			
was good at math when he / she was a child.			

Group literature

Interaction
Group work

Aim
To practice writing, reading and speaking in the present simple, past simple and past progressive tenses.

Time
15–20 minutes

Skills
Writing
Reading
Speaking

Grammar and functions
Review of present simple, past simple and past progressive

Vocabulary
Physical characteristics
Dating

Preparation
Photocopy the worksheets. Make sure you have one for each student in the class.

Procedure

1   Divide the class into groups of six and ask students to arrange their chairs in circles.

2   Explain the task. The students are going to write a story by writing sentences on their worksheets.

3   Give one copy of the worksheet to each student in the class. Ask them to write a boy's name and a brief description of him in the first space provided. Encourage students to include as many details as possible.

4   When that is finished, ask students to fold their paper on the first fold line to hide what they've written. Get them to give their worksheets to the student on their right. The description of the boy should be face down on the desk and the other eight instructions should be face up for the next student.

5   Ask students to write a girl's name and a brief description of her in the space provided. When that is finished, ask them to fold the paper on the second fold line so that both descriptions are now face down on the desk. They should then give this paper to the student on their right.

6   Follow the same steps until all the sentences have been completed.

7   Encourage the students to be creative when they are writing the details. Make sure they cannot see the sentences that other students have already written.

8   When all the sentences have been completed, ask the students to open the completed story they have received and read it aloud to their group.

9   Students could vote for the most interesting story in their groups.

Group literature

Write a boy's name and a description of him.	
Write a girl's name and a description of her.	FOLD
Write where they met.	FOLD
Write what they were doing at the time they met.	
Write his first words to her.	
Write her answer to his first words.	
Write what they did next.	
Write what the neighbors thought about what they did.	
Write where they are and what they're doing now.	

Skyline Resource Pack 2. Published by Macmillan Publishers Limited.

Who is stronger?

Interaction
Whole class

Aim
To compare abilities and physical attributes.

Time
15–20 minutes

Skills
Speaking

Grammar and functions
Comparatives
Asking and answering personal information questions

Vocabulary
General

Preparation
Photocopy and cut apart the cards. Make sure you have one card for each student in the class.

Procedure
1 Give one card to each student in the class.

2 Allow students a minute to familiarize themselves with the information on their cards.

3 Explain the task. Students move around the class looking for three students who have the characteristic or ability listed on their card.

4 Elicit the type of questions students could ask. If necessary, write them on the board, e.g.
How old is your mother?
Can you jump higher than I can? (Both students can jump in the air to see.)

5 Model the activity with one or two students before asking the entire class to start.

6 Set a time limit of ten minutes. Ask students to stand up and begin the activity.

7 While students are gathering information, move around the room and give help if it is needed.

8 When the time is up, invite individual students to report their conclusions to the class. Students should be able to compare themselves with another student, e.g.
Pedro's family is larger than mine. I have one brother. He has three brothers and four sisters!

Option
Ask students to work in pairs instead of as a whole class. Each pair will need a copy of the complete worksheet for this activity. The pairs should compare themselves with regard to all items on the list and write sentences on a separate piece of paper describing the results of their comparisons. They can then report a few of the more interesting conclusions to the rest of the class.

Who is stronger?

Find three people ...

... who are stronger than you are.

... who watch more TV every day than you do.

... who have a larger family than you.

... who can draw a human face better than you can.

... who are younger than you.

... who have longer fingernails than you.

... whose feet are bigger than yours.

... who can count to 20 in English faster than you can.

... whose backpack / purse is fuller than yours.

... whose normal appetite is bigger than yours.

... whose home is larger than yours.

... who are taller than you.

... who can jump higher than you can.

... whose mother is older than yours.

... whose hair is longer than yours.

... whose hands are smaller than yours.

Which one are you going to buy?

Interaction
Pair work
Whole class

Aim
To practice comparing different items.

Time
20–25 minutes

Skills
Speaking

Grammar and functions
Comparatives
Convincing someone of the superiority of a product
Giving reasons

Vocabulary
General

Preparation
Photocopy and cut apart the cue cards. Make sure you have one set (pizza–pizza, car–car) for each pair in the class. If there are more than 14 students in the class, make extra copies, so each extra pair has a matching set of cards. With fewer than 14 students, remove the appropriate number of matching pairs.

Procedure

1 Prepare the students for the activity. Pretend that you're planning your vacation for next month and that you are unsure where to go. Describe the two options, e.g. *going camping with a group of friends* or *going on a package tour to a foreign country.* Ask students to help you make a decision. *Why is one better than the other? What advantages and disadvantages are there?*

2 Ask students to form pairs. Give each pair of students a pair of cards and ask each student in the pair to choose one of the two cards.

3 Explain the task for the first part of the activity.
   • Students should prepare arguments to convince others about their product, e.g. the student with the homemade pizza should prepare an argument to convince the class that homemade pizza is better than frozen pizza. The student with the frozen pizza should prepare an argument that frozen pizza is better than homemade pizza.
   • Set a time limit of five minutes for this part of the activity.

4 Ask students to start and move around the class giving help as needed.

5 When everyone is ready, invite pairs to go to the front of the class and "sell" their products. The rest of the class should listen carefully to the students' arguments and vote for the better product from each pair. Which student was more convincing?

Option
Ask students to work in pairs and write an advertisement for a product so that they can compare their advertisement with that of another pair. Be sure to give out matching pairs of products to the different pairs, e.g. there should be a pair working on a frozen pizza advertisement if there's a pair working on the homemade pizza advertisement. Display the advertisements and vote for the best.

Which one are you going to buy?

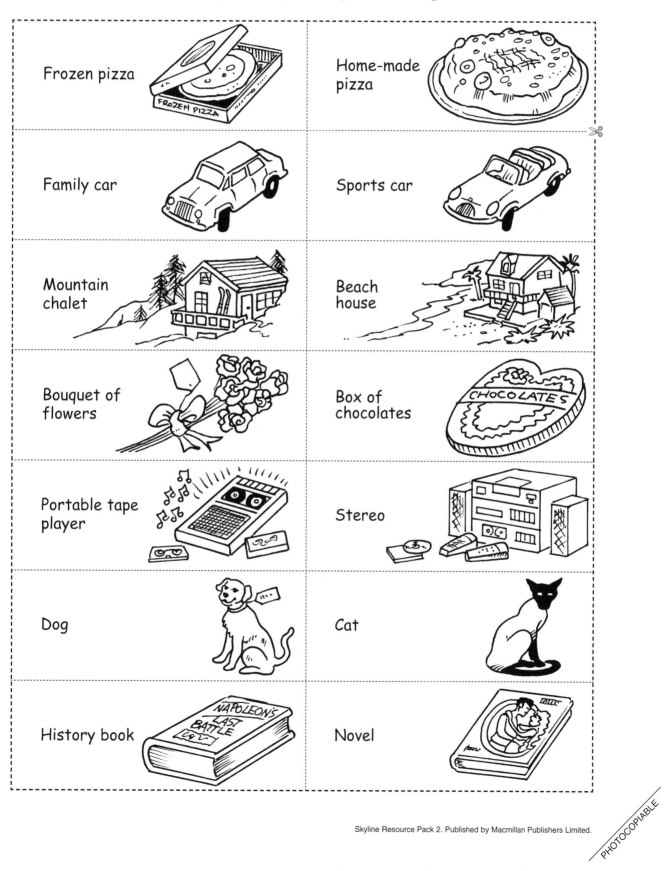

Frozen pizza	Home-made pizza
Family car	Sports car
Mountain chalet	Beach house
Bouquet of flowers	Box of chocolates
Portable tape player	Stereo
Dog	Cat
History book	Novel

Skyline Resource Pack 2. Published by Macmillan Publishers Limited.

Can you do me a favor?

Interaction
Group work

Aim
To practice asking and answering questions using *can* and *could*.

Time
20–25 minutes

Skills
Speaking

Grammar and functions
Asking someone for a favor
Agreeing to do a favor

Vocabulary
General verbs

Preparation
Photocopy and cut apart the cards on the worksheet and shuffle them. Make sure you have one complete set for every group of three students in the class.

Procedure

1   Divide the class into groups of three.

2   Make sure students are aware of the difference between *can* and *could*; i.e. *can* is informal and *could* is formal. If a student asks *Could you open the window please?* then the reply should be quite polite, e.g. *Yes, of course.* or *I'm sorry but I'm afraid I'm busy.* If a student asks *Can you open the window?* then the reply can be more informal, e.g. *Yes, sure. Yes, ok.* or *Sorry, I'm busy right now.*

3   Explain the game.
   • The objective is to collect matching pairs of request and reply cards. Request cards (with sad faces) show actions that need doing and reply cards (happy faces) show the completed action.
   • Students shuffle and distribute all the cards.
   • Students look at the cards in their hands and put any matching pairs they have face up on the table. A matching pair is a card with a request and a card with a reply which are about the same subject.
   • One player starts the game by choosing one of his / her request cards and asking another person in the group the appropriate question, e.g. Look at the card with the dirty dog, ask: *Can you wash the dog?*
   • If the player who is asked the question holds the matching card, he / she should answer *Yes, I can.* He / She should then give that card to the person who made the request and the completed pair should be placed face up on the table.
   • If that player doesn't hold the matching card, he / she should give an excuse such as *I'm sorry, I'm busy right now.*
   • Players can make one request on each turn, regardless of the answer they get.
   • The first player to use all of his / her cards wins the game.

4   Demonstrate the game with a student.

5   Distribute the cards to each group and ask them to begin the game.

6   Walk around the room and give help as needed.

Can you do me a favor?

Incomplete history

Interaction
Pair work

Aim
To practice asking questions using the past simple.

Time
15–20 minutes

Skills
Speaking
Reading

Grammar and functions
Past simple
Asking and answering questions

Vocabulary
General

Preparation
Photocopy and cut apart the A / B cards. Make sure you have a complete A / B set for each pair of students in the class.

Answers

Pedro <u>Álvares</u> Cabral was born in <u>1467</u> and was the third son of Fernão Cabral, Governor of Beira and <u>Belmonte</u>. A friend of Vasco <u>da Gama</u>, he was asked by Manuel I to lead a fleet of <u>13</u> ships going to <u>India</u>. His job was to establish commercial relations and introduce <u>Christianity</u> in the places he visited. The ships left Lisbon on March 9, <u>1500</u> and sailed the seas until, on <u>April</u> 22, they saw a mountain. On April <u>25</u>, they sailed into the harbor called <u>Porto</u> <u>Seguro</u>. Cabral took this land, <u>Brazil</u>, for Portugal and continued his trip on May 3, going this time to the Cape of <u>Good</u> <u>Hope</u>. <u>Four</u> ships were lost in a storm but he eventually arrived in <u>India</u> and returned to Portugal with rich treasures. Later, Cabral retired to his estate in the <u>Beira</u> <u>Baixa</u> province of Portugal and spent his last years there.

Procedure

1 Prepare the students for the activity. Elicit information about Pedro Álvares Cabral by asking questions, e.g. *What do you know about Cabral? What is he famous for? What country did he discover?*

2 You may like to pre-teach the words below.
A fleet – a group of ships sailing together.
To establish – to start a project or relationship.
To sail – to travel in a sailing boat.
A harbor – a place where ships can stay before or after a journey.
A storm – bad weather.
Treasure – a quantity of valuable items, often precious metals or jewels.
To retire – to stop working, usually at about 60 or 65 years old.

3 Give half the class A cards and the other half B cards. Explain that students A and B have different incomplete paragraphs about Cabral and that they need to complete their paragraphs by asking each other questions.

4 Elicit the types of questions they are going to ask, e.g. *When was Cabral born? How many ships were there in his fleet?*

5 If necessary, play the part of a student A and model the activity with a student B.

6 Divide the students into A / B pairs.

7 Set a time limit of ten minutes and ask students to start the activity.

8 When the time is up, check students' answers.

Additional ideas
Ask students to write a short paragraph about a famous person from their city or country. Have them work individually or in groups. Display their work or have a representative from each group read aloud their paragraph.

Incomplete history

Student A

Pedro _____ Cabral was born in 1467 and was the third son of Fernão Cabral, Governor of Beira and _____. A friend of Vasco da Gama, he was asked by Manuel I to lead a fleet of _____ ships going to India. His job was to establish commercial relations and introduce _____ in the places he visited. The ships left Lisbon on March 9, 1500 and sailed the seas until, on _____ 22, they saw a mountain. On April 25, they sailed into the harbor called _____ _____. Cabral took this land, Brazil, for Portugal and continued his trip on May 3, going this time to the Cape of _____ _____. Four ships were lost in a storm but he eventually arrived in _____ and returned to Portugal with rich treasures. Later, Cabral retired to his estate in the Beira Baixa province of Portugal and spent his last years there.

- ✂

Student B

Pedro Álvares Cabral was born in _____ and was the third son of Fernão Cabral, Governor of Beira and Belmonte. A friend of Vasco _____, he was asked by Manuel I to lead a fleet of 13 ships going to _____. His job was to establish commercial relations and introduce Christianity in the places he visited. The ships left Lisbon on March 9, _____ and sailed the seas until, on April 22, they saw a mountain. On April _____, they sailed into the harbor called Porto Seguro. Cabral took this land, _____, for Portugal and continued his trip on May 3, going this time to the Cape of Good Hope. _____ ships were lost in a storm but he eventually arrived in India and returned to Portugal with rich treasures. Later, Cabral retired to his estate in the _____ province of Portugal and spent his last years there.

Do you agree?

Interaction
Whole class

Aim
To practice using superlatives.

Time
20–25 minutes

Skills
Speaking

Grammar and functions
Comparatives and superlatives
Sharing opinions

Vocabulary
General

Preparation
Photocopy the worksheets. Make sure there is one for each student in the class.

Procedure
1   Give each student a worksheet.

2   Explain the task for the first part of the activity. Students read the sentences and fill out the *You* column with their personal opinions.

3   Set a time limit of about five minutes. Ask students to complete the task individually.

4   When the time is up, explain the task for the second part of the activity. Students stand up and move around the room, interviewing three students and filling out the columns *1, 2* and *3* with the answers they receive. Students could put a check if other students agree with them and a cross if other students disagree. If a student agrees with them, they should also add their name or initials. The objective of the activity is for students to find someone who agrees with most of their opinions.

5   Set a time limit of ten minutes. Ask students to start the second part of the activity and move around the room to give help if needed.

6   When the time is up invite individual students to report their conclusions to the class.

Option
Instead of working with the whole class in the second part of the activity, students could be divided into groups of four. Their task would be to find someone in the group who agrees with most of their opinions.

Additional ideas
Do a class survey to find out which items most of the class agree about and which items most of the class disagree about.

Do you agree?

Write the name of ...	You	A	B	C
the worst TV show.				
the most difficult language for you.				
the most important person in history.				
the most exciting job.				
the best place to take a vacation.				
the ugliest city you know.				
the funniest actor or actress.				
the most romantic kind of date.				
the best way to spend a weekend.				
the happiest day of the year.				
the most dangerous place to visit.				
the biggest problem the world faces today.				
the most serious problem a family can have.				
the best song ever written.				
the best athlete.				

Where's the treasure?

Interaction
Group work

Aim
To understand clues and find a hidden object.

Time
20–25 minutes

Skills
Reading

Grammar and functions
Reading and using clues

Vocabulary
Topographical points

Preparation
Photocopy one worksheet for every group of students. Cut apart the clues and separate the card with the answer. Keep this card with you. Write the number of each clue on the back of each clue card. Bring dice and game pieces to the class. Alternatively, have students make dice by using pieces of paper with the numbers 1 to 6 written on. Pieces could be coins or paper clips.

Procedure
1 Divide the class into groups of four or five.

2 Explain the situation. A famous pirate, Captain Williams, buried some treasure on Tihimipu Island before he died. His map and some clues were found in a bottle.

3 Explain the rules of the game.
   • The objective is to find the treasure.
   • Each student should put their game piece on the ship which is the starting point.
   • Each student rolls the dice in turn and moves his / her piece from place to place, according to the number rolled.
   • As students move around the board, they will enter the six places on the island. When students enter a place they can read the clue that has the same number as the place. They should do this silently and note any relevant information. The clue should then be placed face down on the table again. Students should not discuss the information on the cards.
   • When a student thinks he / she knows where the treasure is hidden, he / she should roll the dice and return to the ship, as the answer can only be announced from the ship.
   • Once back at the ship, the student should say where the treasure is. He / She should then raise a hand so you can give him / her the answer card. The student should read the answer silently and say if he / she got the answer correct.
   • If the student got it correct he / she wins the game. If not, he / she must put the answer card face down on the table and say nothing. This student is then out of the game.
   • The rest of the students continue playing until one student discovers where the treasure is hidden.

4 Start the game and walk around the classroom giving help as needed.

Additional ideas
After the game, ask students to write a short paragraph about where the treasure was hidden, giving reasons why it was hidden there.

Where's the treasure?

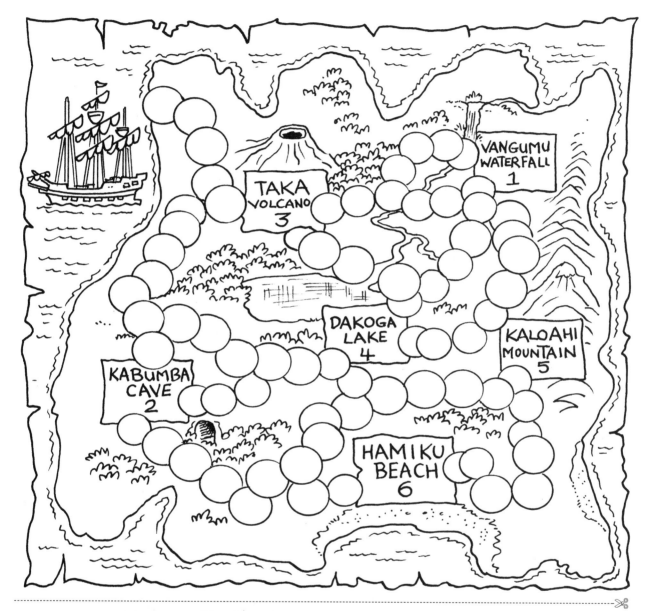

1	2	3	4	5	6	ANSWER
Captain Williams wanted to hide the treasure far away from the salt of the ocean.	Captain Williams grew up near the Atlas Mountains in Morocco.	Taka Volcano erupted three times while Captain Williams was on the island.	Captain Williams wanted to hide the treasure at a high altitude.	Captain Williams was afraid of bats and didn't like dark places.	Captain Williams didn't want the treasure to get wet.	The treasure is hidden on Kaloahi Mountain.

Skyline Resource Pack 2. Published by Macmillan Publishers Limited.

Pictionary

Interaction
Group work

Aim
To review vocabulary learned in this and previous units.

Time
20–25 minutes

Skills
Speaking

Grammar and functions
Guessing or defining words

Vocabulary
General

Preparation
Photocopy and cut apart the cards. Only one set is necessary for the class.

Procedure

1 Divide the class into two teams. If the class is large, divide the class into groups of 6 or 8 and then divide those groups into teams. Play the game in each group simultaneously, so that more students have a chance to participate. (In this case you will need one set of cards for each group.)

2 Explain the task.
   - A student from one team comes to the front of the class, picks up a card from the pile and draws pictures on the board so that his / her team can guess the first word on the card.
   - Students are not allowed to write words but must draw pictures to represent the word.
   - The rest of the team watch the drawing process carefully and try to guess which word is being drawn or represented.
   - The student who is drawing is only allowed to say *Yes* or *No*.
   - There are three words on each card. When one word is guessed, that same student should start drawing the images for the second word, and then the third word.
   - Students have two minutes to get their team to guess all three words.
   - Teams will get one point for each word guessed in the two minutes. The team with the most points at the end of the game is the winner.

3 Demonstrate the game to the students by drawing pictures and having them guess the words.

4 Remind students that someone will time the game. As a member of one team goes to the board, the time manager must set a timer and shout *Time!* after two minutes.

Additional Ideas
Instead of drawing the items on the board, the student at the front of the room can define the words. Team members should guess the words within a time limit of two minutes.

Pictionary

CHEMISTRY	JOGGING	CLASSMATE	AEROBICS
WINDSURFING	HEAVY	DISCO	LIBRARY
CONCERT	MENU	SINGLE	FAX
BEACH	DENTAL FLOSS	CAVITY	BEARD
ENGLISH	BOOKSTORE	PARIS	CAFETERIA
TOOTHACHE	ROCK STAR	MUSEUM	SUN BATHING
KARATE	MODERN	HOTEL	JOB
ARTIST	BRAZIL	FAST FOOD	SPORTS
BRUSH	PASSPORT	BALD	BUS STATION
COFFEE	HISTORY	SINGER	STUDENT
SCIENTIST	GROW	BLOND	CURLY
COCKTAIL PARTY	PLANE	MEXICO	TRAIN
BASKETBALL	HIKING	PRINCIPAL	EXERCISE
TOKYO	SALAD	TENNIS	SHORT
BOSS	PRINTER	MOUNTAIN	FAMILY
TEACHER	GEOGRAPHY	SOCCER	COACH
TOOTHPASTE	HOSPITAL	DENTIST	HAIR
CHINESE	MIDNIGHT	MOON	CONVENTION

Who is it?

Interaction
Pair work

Aim
To practice asking and answering questions about physical descriptions.

Time
15–20 minutes

Skills
Speaking

Grammar and functions
Present simple in *yes / no* questions
Asking and answering questions about people's physical characteristics

Vocabulary
Physical characteristics

Preparation
Photocopy the worksheet. Make sure there is one for each student in the class.

Procedure

1 Give a copy of the worksheet to each student in the class.

2 Divide the students into A / B pairs.

3 Explain the task. Student A chooses a person on the worksheet and student B tries to guess who it is by asking *yes / no* questions. They then change roles.

4 Remind students that they have the right to ask five questions to discover who the person is. If they discover the person after the first question they get 5 points. If they discover the person after the second question they get 4 points. (Third question: 3 points etc.)

5 Elicit the types of questions they are going to ask each other and write them on the board, e.g. *Does this person have a beard? Is it a man? Does she wear glasses?*

6 If necessary, play the part of a student A and model the activity with a student B.

7 Set a time limit of ten minutes and ask students to begin the activity in their pairs.

8 While students are doing the activity, move around the room and give help if it is needed.

9 When the time is up ask students to calculate their scores. The student with the highest score in each pair is the winner.

Option
Students work in groups. Each group chooses a picture and writes a paragraph describing the person's physical characteristics. When they've finished, one person from each group reads the description aloud. The class guesses who is being described.

Who is it?

They need advice!

Interaction
Group work

Aim
To practice giving advice.

Time
20–25 minutes

Skills
Speaking

Grammar and functions
Giving advice
Should / need to

Vocabulary
General

Preparation
Photocopy the game board, one for each group of four or five students in the class. Bring some dice to class (one per group) or prepare small pieces of paper with the numbers 1 to 6 for each group.

Procedure

1 Divide the class into groups of four to five.

2 Ask each student to find something to be used as a game piece like a small paper clip or a pen lid.

3 Tell students they are going to practice giving advice. Give them a situation, e.g.
My friend is too fat and she doesn't feel well.
Elicit some advice, e.g.
She should / needs to go on a diet.
Write students' ideas on the board and emphasize the use of *should* and *need to*.

4 Give a copy of the board game to each group.

5 Explain how to play the game.
   • Students roll the dice in turn and move their pieces along the lines.
   • Every time a student lands on a problem square he / she has to look at the picture and give some suitable advice.
   • The other students in the group then decide if the advice is suitable or not.
   • If the advice is suitable, the student can roll the dice and move forward on his / her next turn. If it is not, he / she returns to the previous square he / she was on and throws again on the next turn.
   • There are rewards and penalties in this game. Rewards allow students to move forward a certain number of squares and penalties force them to go backwards.
   • The winner is the student who reaches FINISH first.

6 Ask students to roll the dice. The student with the highest number starts.

7 Set a time limit of about fifteen minutes and ask students to start playing the game.

8 Move around the room and give help if needed.

9 Stop the activity when the time is up.

Additional ideas
Ask pairs of students to choose one of the situations from the game and prepare a small conversation where they explain the problem and give advice. Pairs then present their conversations to the class.

They need advice!

Have you ever ...?

Interaction
Group work

Aim
To practice using the present perfect with *ever*.

Time
15–20 minutes

Skills
Speaking

Grammar and functions
Present perfect with *ever*
Life experiences

Vocabulary
General

Preparation
Photocopy the worksheet, one for each group of five students in the class. Cut apart the cards.

Answers

Variations are acceptable but the questions students are most likely to ask one another are:
Have you ever traveled to Europe?
Have you ever watched an American football game?
Have you ever visited a museum?
Have you ever been camping?
Have you ever been in love?
Have you ever asked for an autograph?
Have you ever found money?
Have you ever won a trophy?
Have you ever slept in class?
Have you ever seen a ghost?
Have you ever read Shakespeare? or Have you ever read a play by Shakespeare?
Have you ever ridden a horse?
Have you ever taken a cruise?
Have you ever broken a bone? or Have you ever broken your leg?
Have you ever flown in a helicopter?

Procedure

1   Divide the class into groups of four or five.

2   Explain the activity. Each group will receive a set of cards. Each student picks up a card in turn and uses the verb and the picture on that card to ask different members of the group a question. The objective of the game is to find someone who can give an honest affirmative answer to the question.

3   Give an example of what appears on the cards and what questions students could ask, e.g. Write the word *eat* on the board and draw an insect. Ask: *Have you ever eaten an insect?* If a student says *yes*, ask that student further questions to clarify the situation, e.g. *When did you eat an insect? Why?*

4   Give out the sets of cards. Ask students to put them face down on the table and start the game.

5   Walk around the classroom and give help as needed. Encourage students to use this as an opportunity to get to know one another better by asking further questions when possible.

6   Stop the game when the groups have finished asking all their questions.

7   Invite students to report some of their findings about members of their group to the class.

Option
Make the game more competitive. Have students count the number of times each person asks a question before finding an affirmative answer. In this way students will be encouraged to predict potential answers, so that they obtain an affirmative answer more quickly. If a student obtains an affirmative answer on their first question, they win a point. The student with the most points wins the game.

Additional ideas
After playing the game, each student could choose one card which he / she answered affirmatively and write a short paragraph about it.

Have you ever ...?

TRAVEL	WATCH	VISIT
BE CAMPING	BE IN LOVE	ASK FOR
FIND	WIN	SLEEP
SEE	READ	RIDE
TAKE	BREAK	FLY

Bingo!

Interaction
Whole class

Aim
To practice the past participle form of regular and irregular verbs.

Time
15–20 minutes

Skills
Speaking

Grammar and functions
Past participle form of regular and irregular verbs

Vocabulary
Infinitive and past participle form of verbs

Preparation
Photocopy the worksheet, one for each student in the class.

Answers

eaten	studied	ended
risen	needed	broken
bought	looked	said
danced	made	played
thought	worked	drunk
done	run	owned
driven	camped	had
jumped	happened	slept
been	loved	fallen
wished	taken	lived
liked	forgotten	seen
pushed	cooked	attended
swum	ridden	gone
won	gotten	pulled
read	hated	printed
written	climbed	come
hoped	brought	

Procedure

1 Give a worksheet to each student in the class.

2 Tell the students that they are going to play *Bingo* and draw their attention to the list of verbs on their worksheets.

3 Ask students to choose 25 of those verbs and write the past participle form in the *Bingo* squares. They should put a different verb in each square.

4 Check that all the students are clear about the past participle form of verbs. Elicit some examples before they complete their cards, e.g. Teacher: *What is the past participle of see?* Students: *Seen.*

5 When students have completed their cards, explain how to play the game.
   • Tell students that you are going to call out verbs in their infinitive form.
   • The students' task is to look for the corresponding past participle form of those verbs on their bingo cards.
   • If students have the corresponding past participle, they should cross it out.
   • The first student to have all the Bingo squares crossed out wins.

6 Make sure all the students are ready and start calling out the verbs.

7 When a student calls out *Bingo!* have him / her read his / her card aloud so that you can check that all the past participle forms are correct.

Option
Instead of stopping the game after a student has crossed out all the 25 squares on his / her Bingo card, the winner could be the first student to complete five in a line, either vertically, horizontally or diagonally.

Bingo!

eat	do	like	write	make	love	get	break	have	attend
rise	drive	push	hope	work	take	hate	say	sleep	go
buy	jump	swim	study	run	forget	climb	play	fall	pull
dance	be	win	need	camp	cook	bring	drink	live	print
think	wish	read	look	happen	ride	end	own	see	come

Snakes and ladders

Interaction
Group work

Aim
To practice describing experiences in the present perfect.

Time
25–30 minutes

Skills
Speaking

Grammar and functions
Present perfect
Describing experiences

Vocabulary
General

Preparation
Photocopy the board game, one for each group of four students in the class. Bring some dice to class (one per group). Alternatively, you could ask students to write the numbers 1 to 6 on small pieces of paper.

Procedure
1   Divide the class into groups of four.

2   Ask students to find a game piece to be used in the game. This could be a piece of colored paper with their names, a pen lid or a paper clip.

3   Give out the copies of the board game, one to each group of students.

4   Tell students that they are going to play a game called *Snakes and Ladders* and explain the rules of the game.
   - Taking turns, students roll the dice and move their game piece to the correct square.
   - The student reads the instructions on that square and describes an experience he / she has had to the students in the group.
   - There are rewards and penalties in this game. A ladder represents rewards; every time a student lands on a ladder he / she can climb it and move forward a certain number of squares. Snakes represent penalties; every time a student lands on a square with a snake's head he / she must go backwards a certain number of squares, to the end of the tail.
   - The winner is the player who reaches the last square first.

5   Get students to play the game. Students should roll the dice, one at a time. The student with the highest number starts.

Option
Encourage more interaction between the students. When a student lands on a square that asks him / her to describe an experience, you could have the other students ask at least three questions about the experience. This encourages students to listen to the student describing his / her experience and allows all students to participate more.

Snakes and ladders

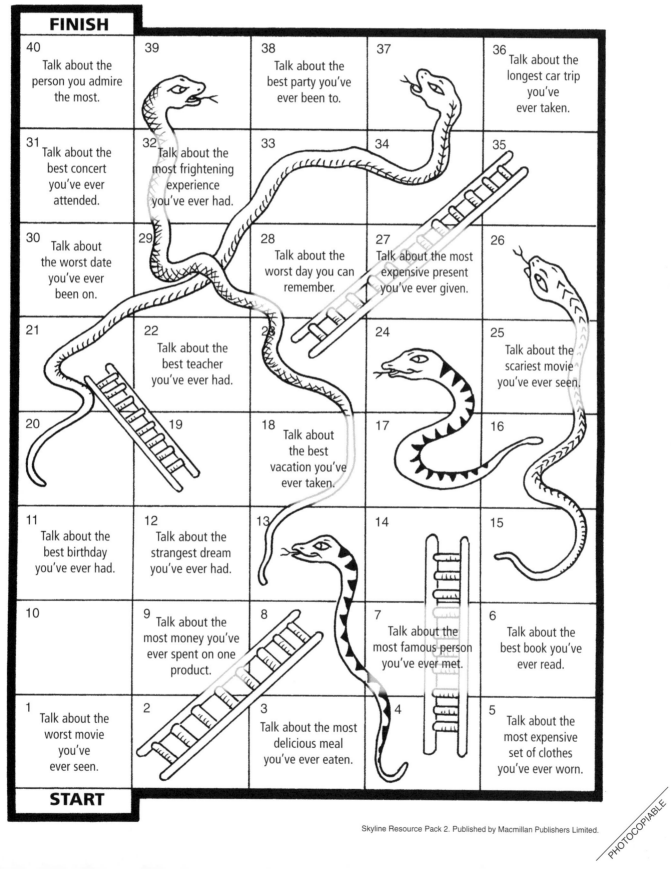

FINISH				
40 Talk about the person you admire the most.	39	38 Talk about the best party you've ever been to.	37	36 Talk about the longest car trip you've ever taken.
31 Talk about the best concert you've ever attended.	32 Talk about the most frightening experience you've ever had.	33	34	35
30 Talk about the worst date you've ever been on.	29	28 Talk about the worst day you can remember.	27 Talk about the most expensive present you've ever given.	26
21	22 Talk about the best teacher you've ever had.	23	24	25 Talk about the scariest movie you've ever seen.
20	19	18 Talk about the best vacation you've ever taken.	17	16
11 Talk about the best birthday you've ever had.	12 Talk about the strangest dream you've ever had.	13	14	15
10	9 Talk about the most money you've ever spent on one product.	8	7 Talk about the most famous person you've ever met.	6 Talk about the best book you've ever read.
1 Talk about the worst movie you've ever seen.	2	3 Talk about the most delicious meal you've ever eaten.	4	5 Talk about the most expensive set of clothes you've ever worn.
START				

Skyline Resource Pack 2. Published by Macmillan Publishers Limited.

Half a crossword

Interaction
Pair work

Aim
To practice giving definitions.

Time
20–25 minutes

Skills
Speaking

Grammar and functions
Questions in the present simple
Defining words

Vocabulary
Words from unit 11

Preparation
Photocopy and cut apart the A / B cards. Make sure you have one card for each student in the class.

Answers

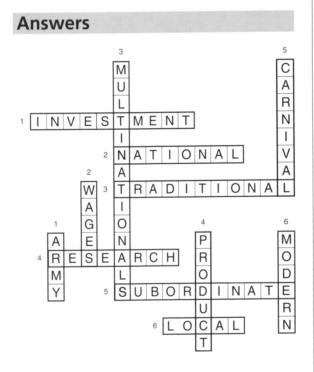

Procedure

1 Give half the class student A cards and the other half student B cards.

2 Divide the students into A / B pairs.

3 Explain the activity. All students have an incomplete crossword puzzle. The task is to complete it by asking their partners for definitions and guessing the word, e.g.
A: *What's number 1 across?*
B: *It's money you put into a bank or project.*
Students should answer by giving a definition. They should not say the word.

4 Ask students to spend a few minutes writing up a definition for each of the six words he / she has on his / her card.

5 When everyone has finished the definitions, set a time limit of about ten minutes and ask students to do the activity.

6 When the time is up or when students have finished, check their answers.

Additional ideas

In pairs or in groups of four or five, ask students to prepare their own crossword puzzle. They can use vocabulary from unit 11 or the entire book. Have them exchange crossword puzzles with another pair or group and complete the new crossword.

Half a crossword

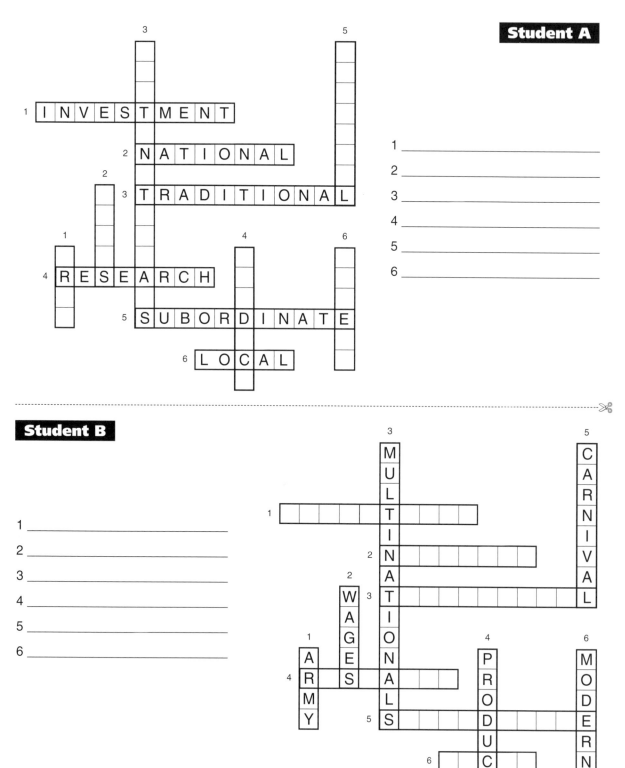

1 _____

2 _____

3 _____

4 _____

5 _____

6 _____

Student B

1 _____

2 _____

3 _____

4 _____

5 _____

6 _____

I've lived here since 1996

Interaction
Group work

Aim
To practice the present perfect with *for* and *since*.

Time
15–20 minutes

Skills
Speaking

Grammar and functions
Present perfect with *for* and *since*
Talking about personal experiences

Vocabulary
General

Preparation
Photocopy the board game, one for each group of four students in the class. Either bring some dice to class or ask students to prepare small pieces of paper with the numbers 1 to 6 written on them.

Procedure

1 Briefly review the use of the present perfect with the students. Write some cues on the board and ask individual students to produce correct sentences, e.g.
travel abroad – 1998
not visit my grandparents – last Saturday
Students should produce sentences, e.g.
I haven't traveled abroad since 1998.
I haven't visited my grandparents since last Saturday.

2 Divide the class into groups of four.

3 Ask students to choose something to be used as game pieces like pen lids or paper clips.

4 Give a copy of the board game to each group.

5 Explain how to play the game.
- Taking turns, students roll the dice and move their game pieces along the board.
- Every time a student lands on a square with a picture, he / she studies the picture and produces a correct sentence using the given verb.
- Sentences should be in the present perfect tense and should include *for* or *since*, wherever possible.
- If the student's sentence is grammatically correct, he / she is allowed to move on on his / her next turn. If it's not, he should stay on that square and try again on his / her next turn.
- There are rewards and penalties in this game. Rewards allow students to move forward and penalties force them to go backwards.
- The first student to reach the last square wins.

6 Have students play the game. Students roll the dice. The student with the highest number goes first.

Option
Extend the game by getting students to ask questions to the person who has given a sentence,
e.g. A: *I've visited Orlando three times since I left school.*
B: *When did you visit? What did you do?*

I've lived here since 1996

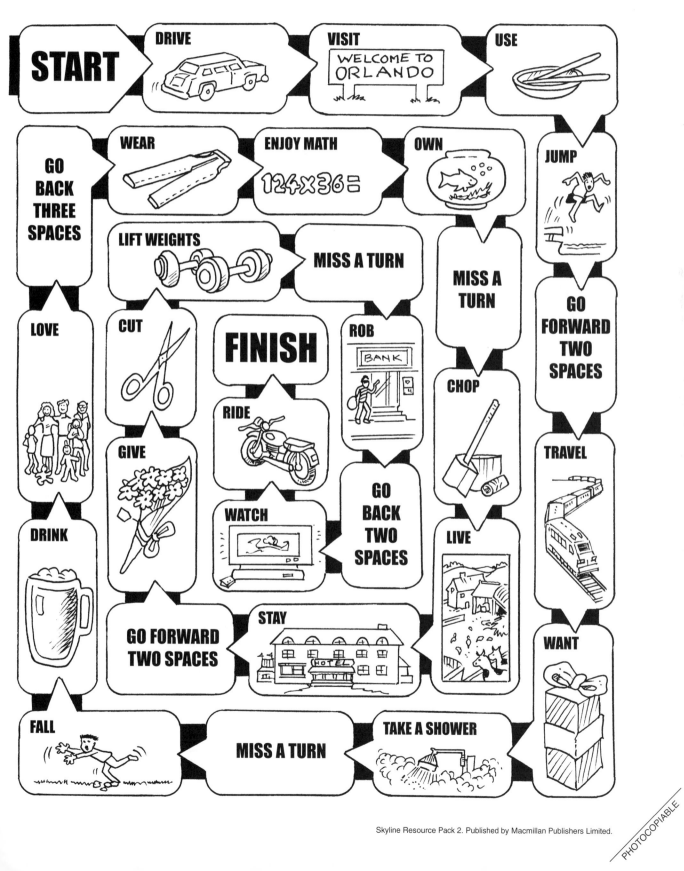

START · **DRIVE** · **VISIT** WELCOME TO ORLANDO · **USE**

GO BACK THREE SPACES · **WEAR** · **ENJOY MATH** 124X36= · **OWN** · **JUMP**

LIFT WEIGHTS · **MISS A TURN** · **MISS A TURN** · **GO FORWARD TWO SPACES**

LOVE · **CUT** · **FINISH** · **ROB** BANK

RIDE · **CHOP** · **TRAVEL**

GIVE · **LIVE**

DRINK · **WATCH** · **GO BACK TWO SPACES**

GO FORWARD TWO SPACES · **STAY** HOTEL · **WANT**

FALL · **MISS A TURN** · **TAKE A SHOWER**

Skyline Resource Pack 2. Published by Macmillan Publishers Limited.

Festival mix up

Interaction
Group work

Aim
To practice reading and recognizing the present and past tenses.

Time
15–20 minutes

Skills
Reading
Speaking

Grammar and functions
Asking and answering about festivals and events

Vocabulary
General

Preparation
Photocopy the worksheet, one for each group of four students in the class. Cut apart the cards in each set and shuffle them.

Answers

The cards are in the correct order on the worksheet.

Procedure

1 Before beginning the activity, talk to the class about local festivals or events from the students' home towns or countries, e.g.
What happens at these festivals?
Why are they popular?
What kinds of food and drink are there?

2 Explain the activity.
   • Students should work in groups of three or four to sort through 12 cards.
   • Four cards contain headlines or titles. Four cards contain brief descriptions of different festivals from around the world and four cards have pictures of the festivals.
   • Students should work together to put the cards into four groups of three cards each. Each group should have a title, a description and a picture.

3 Ask students to form groups of three or four.

4 Distribute the cards.

5 Ask students to begin the activity.

6 Walk around the room giving help when it is needed.

7 When all the groups have finished, check their answers.

8 Students may ask what *O'zapft is!* means. It's German and it means *It's (the beer) been tapped.* It is said by the mayor of Munich when the first keg (barrel) of beer is opened on the first day of the festival.

Option
Ask students to remain in their groups and decide which festival they would enjoy visiting, giving reasons for their choice.

Additional ideas
Ask students to choose a festival they would like to visit and get them to write a short paragraph explaining why that festival interests them.

Festival mix up

"O'zapft is!" Munich's Oktoberfest is fun for the whole family	For over 180 years, the Oktoberfest has been one of Germany's main tourist attractions. For five days in September or October, over six million visitors come to Munich, where they drink nearly six million liters of beer and eat 600,000 roast chickens. There are exciting rides, traditional bands, parades and, of course, plenty of beer. The Oktoberfest is one of Germany's richest traditions and you should visit it if you're near Bavaria in the fall.	
You won't believe your eyes and ears!	The Fourth of July, Independence Day in the U. S., is a big holiday across the entire country. But at State College in Pennsylvania, you can see one of the few truly choreographed fireworks displays in the world – the fireworks are set to music. There's a full day of activities for the whole family including live bands, activities for the kids and even a giant birthday cake. The fireworks display, which takes forty minutes, starts at 9:40 p.m.	
The Battle of Oppikoppi	Do you like fighting and killing? Come to the LAN Fest in Oppikoppi, South Africa for a weekend of death, destruction ... and fun! All you need to bring is your computer with a Network card and a few games like Quake ii & iii and SOF installed and you're ready for war. Participants will set up their computers on Friday and the competition will begin on Saturday, with finals on Sunday. If you think you're good at computer games, come to Oppikoppi and test yourself against the best of the rest.	
Reggae and food donations in Miami	For over seven years, Miami, Florida has been host to the Bob Marley One Love Caribbean Festival. This festival is a day long celebration of music, crafts and art honoring the philosophy and life of Bob Marley, Jamaica's legendary reggae star. Some of the U.S. and Jamaica's top musical acts play at this festival. Since the beginning, the festival has made an effort to feed the hungry, collect canned food and make thousands of dollars for charity.	

Questions in a hat

Interaction
Whole class

Aim
To practice the use of the modal auxiliary *will* to make predictions.

Time
15–20 minutes

Skills
Writing
Speaking

Grammar and functions
Modal auxiliary *will*
Predicting the future

Vocabulary
General

Preparation
Photocopy the worksheet and cut apart the question cards with the empty answer sections attached. Make sure you have two question cards for each student in the class. Remember to bring a hat, a cap or a plastic bag to class.

Procedure
1 Give two question cards to each student.

2 Explain the task for the first part of the activity. Individually, students answer the questions on their cards. Remind students not to write their names on the cards.

3 Set a time limit of five minutes for this part of the activity. When the time is up, collect students' cards and put them in a hat or bag.

4 Explain the task for the second part of the activity. Individually, students stand up and pick one card from the hat / bag. They have to find the person who has written those lines. To do so, students move around the class asking questions. When students find the person who wrote it, they should write the person's name on the card, keep it and pick another card from the hat / bag.

5 Set a time limit of ten minutes and ask students to start the activity.

6 Move around the room and give help if needed.

7 Stop the activity when the time is up.

8 When the game is over, ask students to count how many cards they've collected. The student with the most cards wins.

Option
Photocopy one worksheet for each student in the class. Ask students to form pairs and use these questions as the basis for an interview of one another. They should use the answer section to note down their partner's responses.

Questions in a hat

Questions	**Answers**
What will you do during your next vacation?	_____
Which team will win the next soccer World Cup?	_____
What will be your country's biggest problem in 10 years?	_____
What will you do after class tonight?	_____
Who will be president of your country in 20 years' time?	_____
What will you buy if you become a millionaire?	_____
What will be the next big thing that you buy?	_____
What will you do to keep learning English when you finish this book?	_____
Where will you be in 15 years?	_____
How many children will you have?	_____
What's the best kind of job you'll ever have?	_____
What kind of music will be most popular five years from now?	_____
What will you do when you retire?	_____
What will you do next weekend?	_____
What's the best thing that will happen in your life?	_____
What will the weather be like next weekend?	_____
What's the next movie you'll see?	_____
What will be the hardest thing to teach your children?	_____

I'm sure we've met!

Interaction
Group work

Aim
To practice using the present perfect.

Time
25–30 minutes

Skills
Reading
Speaking

Grammar and functions
Present perfect
Past simple

Vocabulary
General

Preparation
Photocopy the worksheet, one for each group of ten students in the class. Cut apart the cards and shuffle them.

Answers

Marcia Ryan met Phil Stanley in 1942 in Hawaii.

Phil Stanley met John Peterman at Ramsey Accounting and Associates in the 1960s.

John Peterman met Tina Marie Togger in 1979 during the Rocky Mountain forest fires.

Tina Marie Togger met Steve Whitman at Chugwater High School in the 1980s.

Steve Whitman met Miriam Rodriguez in Chicago in the 1990s.

Miriam Rodriguez met Nancy Williams Martinez in Villa Coronado between 1982 and 1984.

Nancy Williams Martinez met Tim Riles at the Michaels & Riles law firm in the 1990s.

Tim Riles met Julia Silvers at the University of Colorado in Boulder several years ago.

Julia Silvers met Tom Lubbock while working for the Boulder police department.

Tom Lubbock met Marcia Ryan recently at the New Home Orphanage in Connecticut.

Procedure

1 Ask students to form groups of ten students. If you have extra students, ask them to work in pairs with another student within the group. Extra students can also form a smaller group. In this case, give each student several identities, making sure that the group has all ten identities in hand when the activity begins.

2 Explain the task.
   • Students should imagine they are at an international conference in St. Louis, Missouri.
   • The students all have different identities and personal histories which they will read about on the cards you give them. They're at the opening cocktail party and each of them recognizes two people.
   • The students' objective is to ask and answer questions until they discover where they've met two of the people before.
   • The students should not let other students read their cards.

3 Shuffle the sets of cards and give one set to each group.

4 Ask students to begin the activity. They should feel free to stand up and change seats as necessary to talk to different members of their group.

5 Move around the classroom giving help as needed.

6 When all students have found both of the people they have met before, stop the activity and check their answers.

Option
Ask students to work in pairs to read the identities and discover who has met whom before. They should then place the ten cards in a circle on their desks to show the chain of connections and underline the phrase in each identity that shows the link between people.

I'm sure we've met!

Marcia Ryan

You were born in Connecticut in 1922 and you went to New York State University for four years to study home economics. You got married in 1942 in Hawaii and moved to California in 1946, after the war. You lived in San Diego for 15 years and then moved back to Connecticut where you worked as a volunteer in the New Home Orphanage for 19 years. You are now retired.

Phil Stanley

You are from Wyoming and you were studying at Colorado University when World War II started. You were transferred to Pearl Harbor in Hawaii in 1941 and stayed there for two years before going to fight in the Pacific. After the war you got married and moved to Parker, Mississippi where you worked for 38 years for Ramsey Accountants. You are now retired and live in Louisville, Mississippi.

John Peterman

You were born in Mississippi. Your first job was in 1965 when you worked as an assistant for Ramsey Accountants but you soon found that you preferred working outside. You took an intensive course with the U.S. Park Services and became a forest ranger in 1970. You moved to Wyoming in 1972 to work in the Rocky Mountains and helped rescue residents of the area during the forest fires of 1979. You now live in Mississippi again and work part-time.

Tina Marie Togger

You've lived all your life in Wyoming and were born in the 1960s. You almost left the state after the forest fires that burned the Rocky Mountains in 1979 but you rebuilt your home and, after getting married, became a teacher at Chugwater High School. You have two children who are now students at Chugwater High School. Last year on your vacation you decided to tour the United States and traveled over 5,000 miles in a camper van.

Steve Whitman

You're originally from Wyoming where you graduated from Chugwater High School in 1989. You then moved to Chicago to work with teenagers with drug problems in the inner cities. You were a counselor in Chicago for 10 years until you met your wife, who comes from Hawaii. You and your wife now live in Honolulu and have two small children, Ben and Emily.

Miriam Rodriguez

A native of Villa Coronado, Mexico, you moved to the U.S. in 1984 and studied psychology at the University of Kansas in Lawrence. After graduation you became a psychologist for the Chicago Public Schools where you specialized in drug addiction and trained counselors for the entire city from 1990 to 1997. You now live in New York City where you work as a psychologist for the New York Public School system.

Nancy Williams Martinez

You were born in 1970 in Honduras. Your father is Mexican and your mother is American and you moved to your father's hometown of Villa Coronado, Mexico in 1982, where you lived for 12 years. In 1994, after studying law for five years at the University of Texas, you moved to Denver, Colorado to work for the Michaels & Riles law firm. Your husband is from Mexico City and you moved back to Mexico two years ago. You now work for a law firm in Oaxaca.

Tim Riles

You were born in 1955 in Tucson, Arizona and went to Kenyon College in Ohio for four years. After finishing your law degree at Stanford University in 1962, you moved to Denver where you opened the Michaels & Riles law firm with your best friend, Craig Michaels. You still work hard but will retire next year and plan to spend more time with your hobby: photography. You've taken several courses at the University of Colorado and hope to sell your work to magazines and newspapers.

Julia Silvers

You have a busy life! You are a full-time freelance photographer and a part-time professor of photography at the University of Colorado in Boulder. You also work part-time as a crime scene photographer for the Boulder police department. Your two children, Lynn and Mark, study at an elementary school in Boulder where you volunteer as an aide in the classroom and your husband, also a professional photographer, works full-time for National Geographic magazine.

Tom Lubbock

You were born in 1960 in Arizona but moved to Nevada two years later with your family. You grew up in Las Vegas and considered working in the casinos. However, one night your family was robbed of all its possessions and you decided to become a detective and work for the police. You took a police training course and worked for the Boulder police department in Colorado for 14 years. You recently moved to Connecticut with your family where you now work in the Hartford Police Department and your wife is director of the New Home Orphanage.

Time travelers

Interaction
Group work

Aim
To practice differentiating between the modal auxiliaries *will* and *might*.

Time
20–25 minutes

Skills
Speaking

Grammar and functions
Modal auxiliaries *will* and *might*
Sharing opinions

Vocabulary
General

Preparation
Photocopy the worksheet, one for each student in the class.

Procedure

1 Tell the students that they are going to travel to two different time periods: the past – 1500 and the future – 2250.

2 For each time period, ask students to decide where they plan to visit, e.g. they may decide that they are going to Brazil in the past and to a distant planet (Mars, Venus) in the future. The entire class should agree on two places that everyone will visit, one in the past and one in the future.

3 Tell students that they will spend two months in each period and ask them to think of what their life will be like and what kind of things they will need. Elicit suggestions around the class, e.g. *I think I'll need a gun in 1500. I might need to hunt for food. I think I'll need a camera in 2250. They might not have cameras and I'll want pictures of my trip.*

4 Explain the task for the first part of the activity. Tell students they can take five objects with them. They should take a look at the list of objects on their worksheets and individually choose five for each period and write them in the appropriate column.

5 Set a time limit of five minutes and ask students do the task individually.

6 When the time is up, ask students to form groups of five.

7 Explain the task for the second part of the activity. Students should discuss their ideas with the group and make a group list of five objects and write them in the appropriate column.

8 Set a time limit of about ten minutes for this part of the activity. When the time is up, ask one person from each group to report the conclusions of his / her group to the class.

Additional ideas
Groups could discuss their ideas and make a class list.

Time travelers

The year 1500

	You	Group
1		
2		
3		
4		
5		

The year 2250

	You	Group
1		
2		
3		
4		
5		

Objects

a knife	scotch tape	a clock	some seeds	your passport
a copy of the constitution of your country	a CD player and CDs	your best friend	soap	a lawyer
a computer	a pen and paper	a horse and saddle	the Bible	an encyclopedia
a recipe book	an atlas	a good book	beautiful necklaces	a bottle of vodka
a camera	pictures of your family	a dictionary	pictures of your city	some matches
a gun	some gold bars	a bus and gasoline	water	warm clothes
medicine	a fork and spoon	some basic food	hand grenades	cigarettes

Macmillan Education
Between Towns Road, Oxford OX4 3PP
A division of Macmillan Publisher Limited
Companies and representatives throughout the world

ISBN 0 333 92679X

Designed and illustrated by Red Giraffe

Cover photograph by Stone

Printed in Hong Kong

2005 2004 2003
10 9 8 7 6 5 4 3 2